A REVOLUTION

TO WIN

The Founders' Solution

to the Present Crisis

Roger K. Rutledge

Evelyn Press

ISBN-13: 978-1478154082

Political Science / Government / Legislative Branch

Manufactured in the United States of America

TABLE OF CONTENTS

.

To the memory of J.P. Rutledge, Jr., a quiet hero,
my father, best friend, mentor, and partner
in the practice of law.

PREFACE

The seed for this book was planted twenty-five years ago, in the course of a family vacation to Washington, D.C. We went to the National Archives to see the originals of the great founding documents. Reprints of the original documents were on sale, and I bought several of them to frame and hang in the conference room of my law office in Memphis, Tennessee. Among them was an exact reproduction of the Bill of Rights, which I had known since taking civics in high school as the first ten amendments to the United States Constitution. These are the amendments which secured the great freedoms of speech, religion, the press, assembly, to bear arms, and guaranteed the rights of citizens against unlawful arrest, search and seizure, detention, cruel and unusual punishments, and the like.

One day, while reading the framed Bill of Rights on the wall of my conference room, I noticed that the original Bill of Rights consisted not of ten proposed amendments, but twelve. The reproduction from the National Archives bore a note that, although the original Bill of Rights contained twelve proposed amendments, only ten of them were ratified by the thirteen States of the new nation. This drew my attention to the two proposed amendments which had not been ratified. One of them is now familiar, because it provides that no pay raise for members of Congress shall take effect until commencement of the term of Congress next following approval of the pay raise. This very amendment was ratified by approval of three-fourths of the States 203 years later, in 1992, as the Twenty-seventh Amendment to the United States Constitution, the most recent Constitutional amendment to be adopted.

The remaining unratified amendment proposed in the Bill of Rights prescribed how many Representatives were to be elected to the House of Representatives as the nation's population increased. I have pointed out to many clients and acquaintances over the years this proposed amendment and have talked about what our national government would be like today if it had been ratified as intended. The people with whom I discussed it generally felt that the country would be better off today if the intent of this amendment had been fulfilled. This is the subject which I present for your consideration in this book.

INTRODUCTION

A CALL TO REVOLUTION

Americans today are passing through a time of trial. People of every class and persuasion are troubled. Our economy is not working. People fear losing their jobs. Homes are being lost to foreclosure. Billions are spent on military adventures while basic needs go unmet at home. Debt has spiraled out of control. Grid lock grips the government. A nasty spirit of partisan bickering spoils political discussion. Elected officials seek division instead of consensus. People in positions of authority lord it over others. Waste and corruption taint public administration at every level. Greed infects big business. The average person feels left out and powerless to do anything about it.

How did we get to this point? What can we do about it? Politicians and candidates for office propose solutions in the form of programs. Such measures only treat the symptoms. They do not reach the root cause of the problem. Demonstrators occupy Wall Street and raise protests in cities across America. Tea Party organizers mount similar protests against the status quo. Despite their differences in thinking, these dissidents have much in common and give a voice to the discontent felt by many. However, they have no real solutions, no agenda, and no goal. Most people are silent, fearful, worried, even alarmed at the course of events.

Deep historic currents have brought us to this point. To meet the challenge of the present situation, we must first understand how we got here. We must understand the problem and its consequences. Then we must have the courage to solve it. There is a solution. It will take nothing less than a revolution. This revolution is not new. It has been around for 223 years. It is, literally, a revolutionary idea forged in the first struggle of the American Revolution and its aftermath.

CHAPTER ONE

THE PROBLEM

Simply stated, the problem boils down to this: *concentration of power in the hands of a few.*

The American system of government is laid out in the Constitution of the United States. The framers of the Constitution chose to adopt a republican form of government consisting of (a.) a legislative branch made up of elected representatives, (b.) an executive branch made up of an elected president and vice-president, and (c.) a judicial branch made up of Supreme Court justices and federal judges selected by the executive branch subject to the approval of the legislative branch. This division of governmental functions was intended to prevent a concentration of power in any one branch by means of a system of checks and balances among the three branches of the government. In this respect it works amazingly well.

The legislative branch consists of two houses or chambers, the Senate and the House of Representatives. The Senate represents the various States in the United States, each of which elects two senators. The House of Representatives represents the people; in fact, it is the only federal governmental body whose members are directly elected by the people.[1] Each State elects a certain number of Representatives based upon its population taken from the Census every ten years. Together, the Senate and House of Representatives are referred to as the United States Congress.

The House of Representatives is the only body in the government which can initiate taxation and spending. This is the "power of the purse." It also adopts legislation affecting commerce, as well as other laws considered to promote the health, safety, and welfare of the people. The House of Representatives can declare war and provide for the armed forces to wage war. These are enormous powers which directly affect every citizen.

When the Constitution was first adopted, there had not yet been a census. The number of Representatives in the first United States Congress (which convened in 1789) was set at twenty-one members. This was one Representative for every 187,110 people, and was increased to twenty-six, or one Representative for every 151,127 people. After the first Census in 1790, the number was determined according to Article I, Section 2, Clause 3 of the United States Constitution which states:

> Representatives and direct Taxes shall
> be apportioned among the several

---

[1] Even though the President is generally considered to be elected by the people, the vote is actually taken from electors who are selected by popular vote at the State level. The people elect Senators, but they represent States (each has two) and are not elected on the basis of population.

States which may be included within this Union, according to their respective Numbers, which shall be determined by adding to the whole Number of free Persons, including those bound to Service for a Term of Years, and excluding Indians not taxed, three fifths of all other Persons. The actual Enumeration shall be made within three Years after the first Meeting of the Congress of the United States, and within every subsequent Term of ten Years, in such Manner as they shall by Law direct. The number of Representatives shall not exceed one for every thirty Thousand, but each State shall have at Least one Representative; and until such enumeration shall be made, the State of New Hampshire shall be entitled to chuse *[sic]* three, Massachusetts eight, Rhode-Island and Providence Plantations one, Connecticut five, New-York six, New Jersey four, Pennsylvania eight, Delaware one, Maryland six, Virginia ten, North Carolina five, South Carolina five, and Georgia three.

This constitutional provision did not set a fixed number for determining how many Representatives will go to Congress. It provided for the number to be derived from Census data as part of the apportionment process, with a limit that the House membership cannot exceed the number of members which would result in one Representative for every thirty thousand persons. As the population of the United States increased, so did the number of Representatives. After each Census, the number of Representatives was adjusted to enlarge the Congress in proportion to the population. This continued until 1929, when the number of Representatives in the House of Representatives was fixed at 435 members.

The Fourteenth Amendment to the Constitution, in Section 2, altered Article I, Section 2, Clause 3, quoted above. Section 2 of the Fourteenth Amendment states simply that, "Representatives shall be apportioned among the several States according to their respective numbers, counting the whole number of persons in each State, excluding Indians not taxed." By law in 1940, all Indians were subjected to taxation, so that the entire population of each State is now taken into account.

The method by which this number was fixed at 435 was legislative; Congress simply passed a law in 1929 setting the number of Representatives. At the time of the 1930 Census, the population of the United States was 123,202,624 people. This meant that each Representative had some 283,224 constituents, more or less. In the 82 years since passage of the Apportionment Act of 1929, the population of the United States has grown by some 185,542,914 people to 308,745,538 in 2010. Since the total number of Representatives remains the same as in 1929, a Representative today has some 709,760 constituents, more or less depending how districts in each State are reapportioned. This average constituency is almost three times as many as in 1929.

This change in proportion between total Representatives and population has resulted in a tremendous concentration of power in the hands of a few people. To put this in perspective, if the proportion of Representatives to population in 1791 had been what it is today, the 3,929,214 persons counted in the first Census would have had just six Representatives in the House! To view it from another perspective, if the proportion of Representatives to population were today the same as in 1791, the total members now in Congress would be 2,043, not 435. This illustrates the problem which is troubling Americans today: *concentration of power in the hands of the few*. The consequences flowing from this problem are numerous and far reaching.

Federal Hall in New York City,
Where the First U.S. Congress Convened, 1789
(Library of Congress)

CHAPTER TWO

CONSEQUENCES

No one is to blame for our current predicament. Neither Democrats nor Republicans, the rich nor the poor, nor any special interest group caused the problem. It is the natural result of events unfolding in history.

The increasing concentration of power in the hands of a few has coincided with major economic and social changes in America. Principal among these have been (a.) the emergence of the corporation as the primary form of business organization in America, (b.) the enactment of the income tax, and (c.) the intervention of government in the economic life of the country following the Great Depression.

❖ *Corporations*

Beginning in the late 1800's and continuing into the 1920's, the economy of the United States came to be dominated by large corporations. The corporation as a form of business organization had been around since the 1700's and has been described by one legal writer as a "money pump." The corporation is unsurpassed as a mechanism for raising large amounts of capital for business enterprises. Here again, however, tremendous economic power is concentrated in the hands of the few. Tens and hundreds of millions of dollars raised from the sale of stock on the national exchanges spurred the euphoria and wild speculation of the "Roaring Twenties." The extent of this concentration of capital in the hands of corporate management can be seen in the effect of the disaster known as the Great Depression on the lives of ordinary people. "Brother Can You Spare a Dime" became the top popular song of the day.

❖ *The Income Tax*

In 1913, the Sixteenth Amendment to the Constitution was adopted, authorizing Congress to levy an income tax on individuals and businesses in the United States. Before the income tax, the federal government derived most of its revenue from duties, fees, and licenses. These sources funded a modest national budget. With the income tax, the federal budget grew exponentially. In 1918, the federal government for the first time in the history of the country collected more than a billion dollars in revenue. By 1945, tax revenues had increased to an annual amount of 43 billion dollars. According to the Congressional Budget Office, the federal government collected tax revenues totaling 2.3 *trillion* dollars in 2010, 47% of it from the income tax. This is an enormous sum of money, and the power to initiate laws which determine how it is spent rests solely in the hands of the 435 members of the House of Representatives.

❖ *Government Economic Intervention*

In 1929, passage of the Apportionment Act

fixing the number of Representatives at 435 coincided with the stock market crash which precipitated an economic spiral downward, plunging the United States into the Great Depression. This led in 1933 to the election of Franklin Delano Roosevelt as President on the platform of the New Deal.

Prior to Roosevelt's New Deal, the preferred economic policy of government was *laissez faire*: leave the capitalist economic system alone to function without governmental interference. The marketplace was believed to be self-correcting. After the crisis of the Great Depression and the New Deal response to it, *laissez faire* economics was abandoned forever. The New Deal put in place numerous governmental agencies and programs designed to intervene in, stimulate, and regulate economic activity. This trend has continued to the present day.

❖ *The Rise of Special Interest Politics*

The growth of corporations, enactment of the income tax, and adoption of New Deal programs spurred the growth of special interest politics in America. The practice of using agents in Washington to influence the passage of legislation, known since the early days of the republic as "lobbying," mushroomed after these stimuli were introduced. Lobbyists hung around the lobbies of the chambers where Congress met, trying to get the ear of key legislators to support particular proposed laws or bills before the House or Senate.

Lobbying has a long history in the United States and is protected by the free speech guarantees of the First Amendment to the U.S. Constitution. The negative and corrupting potential of this way of influencing government has long been recognized. Attempts to control it have largely failed. As power has become increasingly concentrated in Congress, the impact of lobbying on government has grown.

Lobbying serves the purposes of special interest politics. The legislative decision making process in the United States government is driven by special interest politics. This is how it works. The collection of revenues in the trillions through direct income taxation and fees each year creates what might be called an enormous "money pie" in Washington. Because it holds the power of the purse, each year the House of Representatives (with Senate collaboration) gets to decide how the pie is to be cut. Any individual, association, group, or corporation interested in getting a slice of the pie seeks to influence legislation in the House of Representatives on behalf of their "special interest." Because of their great economic leverage, corporations, trade associations, labor unions, and those involved in the banking and finance industries are the major players in Congressional hearings and lobbying.

As we have seen, the New Deal ushered in policies of intervention by the government in economic life, using the authority of the commerce clause in the Constitution (providing for Congress to pass all laws regulating commerce among the States).

Since the New Deal era, the process of government typically involves introduction and passage of laws and regulations which have the effect of favoring some and disfavoring others financially. Organizations representing special interests are focused on the annual pie cutting which takes place in the House of Representatives. It is not unusual for the lobbyists themselves to draft the proposed laws which are then submitted to Congress by sponsoring Representatives with whom they are friendly.

Lobbyists commit major resources to sponsoring or opposing laws and regulations on a daily basis. These resources include media campaigns and financial contributions channeled to political parties and candidates, as well as gifts, VIP privileges, and entertainment to Representatives and their staff members, families, and friends. A Representative elected to Congress and his or her colleagues become the center of attention from these special interests.

Take a walk around Washington, D.C. The buildings and architecture are impressive. You will find primarily three types of structures: (a) governmental buildings and monuments; (b) foreign embassies; and (c) buildings owned by corporations, associations, organizations, and foundations whose main purpose is to influence Congress on behalf of their special interests. Just about everyone in Washington, regardless whether Republican or Democrat, liberal or conservative, Christian, Muslim, or Jew is a member of just one party: we might call it the Pie Party. Each year they or their agents seek to get in on the party and have their piece of the pie.

What is happening here? The political elite in Washington has hijacked the ship of state! How can a Representative have the interests of his or her constituents at heart while taking large sums of money from special interests? Who claims most of the attention of legislators every day? Political operatives, members of the media and lobbyists who, like the members of Congress themselves, belong to the Washington elite: the Pie Party. Regardless of what they say about positions and issues, they have one thing in common: they buy into the Pie Party. The so-called "national issues" of the special interests override the interests and issues of the people back home.

Never has the problem been more obvious than in laws relating to the banking and finance industry. Congress in our time dismantled laws and regulations enacted after the Great Depression of 1929 which put in place limitations on the activities of banks, stock brokerage companies, and other financial institutions. The banking and financial industry is the largest segment in the American economy today, larger even than the manufacturing sector in asset value. In the 1980's and 1990's brokerages and banks promoted the idea that the Depression era restraints hurt the growth of business capital and were not needed anymore. These firms brought enormous lobbying pressure to bear on the House of Representatives to do away with or loosen regulatory laws constraining their activities. In 1999, Congress repealed the Glass-Steagall Act of 1933, removing the last of these restraints and allowing banks to engage in the business of trading securities.

Soon banks were merging with brokerages and investment firms. They quickly became involved in the business of "securitizing" debt obligations by creating paper certificates called "derivatives." Made up of mortgage debt based on high risk sub-prime loans, these junk securities generated high profit margins on paper and were traded in ever enlarging numbers. By 2008, their activities created a perfect storm for financial meltdown on Wall Street. When it hit, Congress was confronted with a stark choice: allow the banks to fail and risk a downward spiral to depression, or bail them out with taxpayers' dollars. Congress, fearing economic collapse at the moment of truth, sold out Main Street in favor of Wall Street. In the aftermath, calls for reform of the financial sector have been completely frustrated by intense lobbying, resulting in more toothless attempts at legislation which fails to address the systemic problems which caused the crisis. Once again, Congress has sold out Main Street in favor of Wall Street. This was just one of many instances in which corporate executives have enjoyed taxpayer funded "bail outs" rather than facing the consequences of their failures and misdeeds.

Let's look at some of the other consequences of this situation:

❖ *Runaway Spending and Debt*

Power in Washington is a money game. This drives the impulse of Members of Congress to support legislation which authorizes spending money which the government does not have. An example is military spending. No less a military man than former President Dwight Eisenhower warned Americans against the growing influence of the military-industrial complex.[2] Defense contractors and their cronies in the Department of Defense and the House of Representatives use every tactic available to extract billions of dollars from Congress for development of weapons systems and supply contracts. In the same way Congress has enacted

---

[2] In his farewell address after two terms as President, Eisenhower said, "This conjunction of an immense military establishment and a large arms industry is new in the American experience. The total influence – economic, political, even spiritual – is felt in every city, every State house, every office of the Federal government. We recognize the imperative need for this development. Yet we must not fail to comprehend its grave implications. Our toil, resources and livelihood are all involved; so is the very structure of our society.

In the councils of government, we must guard against the acquisition of unwarranted influence, whether sought or unsought, by the military-industrial complex. The potential for the disastrous rise of misplaced power exists and will persist."

Compare this to George Washington's Farewell Address, in which he warned Americans against the danger of maintaining a standing army in peacetime.

back door spending through manipulation of the tax code, subsidies, and other legislative programs which steadily consume money regardless of whether the government has it to spend. Social Security and Medicare, which are not "entitlement programs" because they were set up to be self-funded by contributions from working people out of their paychecks, have fallen prey to the practice of borrowing from these "trust funds" to pay for programs enacted by Congress without regard to available revenue.

❖ *Disempowerment of the People*

Large numbers of Americans today feel disfranchised; they feel their vote means nothing. In a sense, this is true. Whomever they vote into office for the House of Representatives, whether Democrat or Republican, eventually becomes a member of the Pie Party. The interests and concerns of corporate America become the main focus of the Representative's activity. Lobbyists for special interests wine and dine the Representative, whose greatest concern is to raise enough funds to get reelected. The average political campaign for election to Congress in 2008 cost $1.1 million. This was the price of trying to reach voters in a district of some 660,000 people. In short, politics has become a money game in the House of Representatives.

Why do incumbents in Congress tend to get reelected? They have the inside track in the money game. The same thing happens in families. The son or daughter of a Senator or Representative has access to the contacts and financial means to get elected to office. More often than not they succeed. In this way the elite class perpetuates itself and becomes further isolated from the people. America today is in danger of establishing an oligarchy of influential families based on such entrenched privilege and wealth.

This disempowerment of the average citizen produces apathy and alienation in our political system. Apathy is evident in low voter turnout for elections. Typical voter turnouts for mid-term elections for the House of Representatives run between thirty and forty percent. The 2008 election, bolstered by the Obama-McCain presidential campaign, produced an extraordinary sixty-three percent voter turnout. Between 1960 and 1995, voter turnout for elections to the House of Representatives averaged forty-eight percent. These figures reflect that barely half those who bother to register to vote actually participate in elections. Many more adult Americans entitled to vote are not even motivated to register.

People who believe their votes are meaningless simply do not bother to vote. Politics in America has increasingly become an activity of the few because so many people feel their votes make no difference. If the system is self-perpetuating and those who participate in it one way or another belong to the Pie Party, what difference does a vote really make?

❖ *Alienation*

When people feel left out of the process, they eventually begin to feel alienated. They are not part of the discussion. Politics is the game of a privileged, moneyed elite. The discussion does not involve ideas and it does not include, for the most part, ordinary citizens. It is staged elsewhere. Washington and the Pie Party are a million miles away from Main Street, the place where most Americans work and dwell. The sums of money involved are astronomical to the average American. A growing "we - they" spirit widens the gulf between the people and their so-called "elected officials."

❖ *A Growing Gap Between Rich and Poor*

Because politics in Washington has become a money game, it favors the rich over the poor. No special interest group is going to gain any economic advantage from advocating laws and supporting candidates favoring poor people. The so-called "social safety net" exists only to the extent necessary to stave off unrest among the masses who might otherwise threaten the privileged and moneyed interests, and the net is in tatters. It takes money to influence elections and legislation. The motive for doing so is, quite simply, economic advantage. Lobbying Congress to pass laws which favor the poor and disfavor those who enjoy wealth and privilege presents no opportunity for economic gain. Consequently the gap between the rich and the poor is steadily growing wider in this country.

Census Bureau figures show that the gap between rich and poor has been growing for decades. During this period some five percent of annual national income has shifted from the middle class to the richest households in America. The 5,934 wealthiest households in America received 650 billion dollars

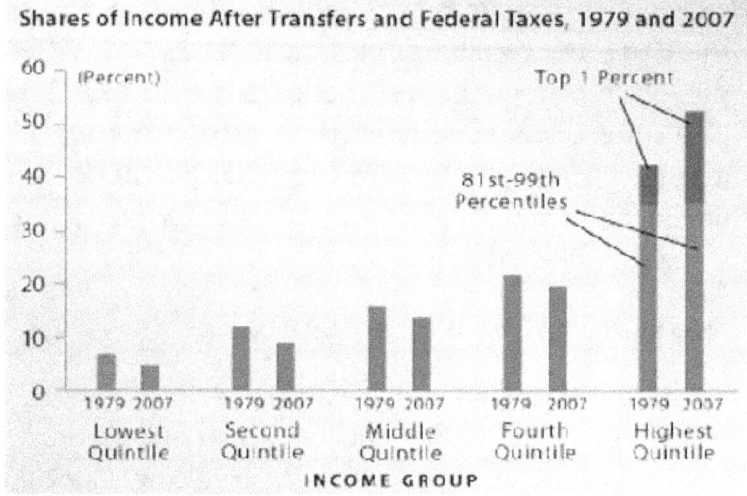

The Growing Income Gap 1979 - 2007
(Source: Congressional Budget Office)

more income in 2010 than they would have had if the economic pie had been divided as it was in 1980. This comes to about 109 million dollars more for each of the richest households in America. In contrast, the U.S. Government reported in 2011 that fifty percent of American workers earned less than $26,364 in 2010.

With rising unemployment, overall pay was trending down except for the wealthiest Americans.

Payroll data derived by the Social Security Administration from W-2 forms submitted to the Internal Revenue Service showed that in 2010, despite the economic crisis which gripped the country, the number of people making a million dollars or more actually increased by more than eighteen percent over 2009. The widening of the gap between rich and poor, fostered by the politics of the Pie Party, actually accelerated after the economic crisis hit in 2008.

The manipulation of tax laws and other legislation to favor the rich threatens to turn America into a land of "haves" and "have-nots." Not only is the poverty of the lower class growing, but the middle class is shrinking. Two of the major findings in a comprehensive study published by Stanford University in November 2011, based on Census Bureau data on incomes and where people live, were summarized as follows:

> 1. From 2000 to 2007, family income segregation grew significantly in almost all metropolitan areas (in 89 percent of the large and moderate-sized metropolitan areas). This extends a trend over the period 1970-2000 during which income segregation grew dramatically. In 1970 only 15 percent of families were in neighborhoods that we classify as either *affluent* (neighborhoods where median incomes were greater than 150 percent of median income in their metropolitan areas) or *poor* (neighborhoods

where median incomes were less than 67 percent of metropolitan median income). By 2007, 31 percent of families lived in such neighborhoods;

and

2. The affluent are more segregated from other Americans than the poor are. That is, high-income families are much less likely to live in neighborhoods with middle- and low-income families than low-income families are to live in neighborhoods with middle- and high-income families. This has been true for the last 40 years. [3]

Economic inequality flows directly from Pie Party politics in Washington. What previously went on mostly behind closed doors is now glaringly apparent. In the wake of the economic crisis, banks, insurance companies, and corporations which have failed to compete effectively in the world economy have gone to Washington and received billions of dollars in bail-outs. Ordinary working Americans get no bail-outs and are left to fend for themselves. Corporate officers and directors shamelessly accepted bonuses funded with money collected from tax revenues. Wall Street money managers who deserved to be fired for irresponsibly trading up junk securities were rewarded while workers who have no

---

[3] *Growth in the Residential Segregation of Families by Income, 1970-2009,* Sean F. Reardon and Kendra Bischoff (Stanford University, November 2011).

lobby in Washington were laid off or forced to accept pay cuts. There is no bail out program for average American workers. When they have to file for bankruptcy, no government plan will rescue them from the disaster.

❖ *Decline in Civility*

The spectacle of easy money going on at the highest levels of government and business makes ordinary people cynical. How can citizens maintain a positive attitude when it is so obvious that Congress is more concerned with what is good for political and corporate operators than what is good for ordinary people back home? The old assumption that "what is good for General Motors is good for America" has been blown away by recent events. The House of Representatives has taken on so much debt to bail out big business (including General Motors) that ordinary Americans will be saddled with it for generations.

The disappointment and frustration felt by the average American finds expression in anger and sarcasm. When money drives politics, as it does in the House of Representatives, partisans dig in to fight for their piece of the pie. Rather than seeking common ground, Representatives nowadays indulge in strident discord. Each side tries to blame the other for what is going on. The American people, however, see both sides as Tweedle Dum and Tweedle Dee. They find no real difference between them, except to the extent that they respond to different special interests.

The nastiness and stridency which characterizes national politics today has a trickle down effect. People begin to act the same way toward one another in school board meetings and city councils. Some people think that it is appropriate to act that way because political candidates and members of Congress act out in that way. This is a grievous departure from the mutual respect that marks American self-government and culture at its best. It is the natural result of debasing public service, reducing it to a Pie Party.

❖ *The Revolving Door*

One of the persistent problems with Washington politics is the revolving door between government and corporate America. Washington is full of well heeled former Congressmen and staff members who serve as consultants for corporations seeking government money and advantages. A favorite technique for years has been to use friends and cronies inside Congress to pepper proposed laws with "earmarks." These specific designations of budgeted funds which go to favored private companies were written into major legislation the House of Representatives was likely to approve. Because such laws are likely to pass without major revision, they become "Christmas trees" for special interests and those who want funding for their pet projects. In 2010 the House Appropriations Committee, in response to criticism of such blatant opportunism, adopted rules to ban earmarks benefiting for-profit corporations. We can be sure that lobbyists are devising ways to use nonprofit corporations and other schemes to dodge the new rules.

Washington consultants have earned fees in the millions in exchange for their sponsorship of clients' earmarks. They occupy lavish offices and enjoy expensive lifestyles funded by feeding from the public trough in this way. They haunt the halls of Congress, as do registered lobbyists, using their contacts to feather their own nests. No one is concerned about the interests of the people back home when they do this. It is a crass pursuit of money, purely and simply. It is one of the ways in which the Pie Party works.

Often corporations hire former members of Congress outright, putting them on the payroll to manage projects on which their contacts and "profile" can be valuable assets. Similarly, members of Congress make contracts hiring business "experts" to fulfill investigative or legislative functions inside Congress. Often they sponsor or approve of the engagement of corporate leaders to serve as heads of government departments, agencies, and commissions. Many of the people brought into government to "solve" the recent financial crisis came to Washington from Wall Street and corporate America. Some were themselves the very financial managers who were involved in carrying out the shady — and greedy — investment and business practices which triggered the crisis in the first place.

A former Speaker of the House of Representatives, Thomas "Tip" O'Neill of Massachusetts, was famous for saying, "All politics is local." This may have once been true, but not anymore. Politics in the House of Representatives is national. Local interests are represented mainly in the arena of constituent services, where staffers assist citizens with problems like getting benefits to which they are entitled from the government. When it comes to lawmaking, it is a battle of titans on the national level. Local interests take a back seat or are forgotten altogether.

Just to put this in perspective, consider the amounts of money reported to be spent on lobbying Congress, especially the House of Representatives. In the last three years, lobbying Congress and federal agencies has become a $3.5 billion industry annually. Since we have only 435 Representatives, this means lobbyists are spending millions per Congress member in seeking to directly influence legislation in the House. Is it any wonder that the average American feels disfranchised and left out of this insiders' game?

Before going on, it needs to be said that there is no reason to make villains of the people in Washington and in corporate America who are doing this. They are only doing what comes naturally, what virtually anyone might do under the same circumstances. Power corrupts, and concentrating power in the hands of a few is very corrupting. The problem is in the *system*. We must remind ourselves, however, that in America ultimate political power rests in the hands of the people. It is up to the people to change the system. Otherwise, the inside operators in Washington and on Wall Street and in the corporate board rooms of America will simply keep doing what comes naturally, and Pie Party politics will continue.

❖*Decline in Ethics*

Americans at the dawn of the new millennium have witnessed unprecedented corruption in government and business. Congress is the focal point. Under pressure from corporations and the financial industry, Congress has relaxed legislation which provided regulation and oversight on Wall Street, forgetting the lessons of history. Corporate money managers and traders escaped the scrutiny of regulators through their ability (bestowed by Congress) legally to generate money using sub-prime lending, creation of "derivatives" and junk bonds, and other forms of so-called investment that converted shaky mortgage loans and other debt obligations into securities to be traded in "hedge funds." When the underlying debt obligations fell into default, millions of dollars evaporated from investment bank balances sheets, plunging the nation into crisis.

This environment of unchecked power concentrated in the hands of the few made it easy for brokers and money managers to squander the financial resources of ordinary people while living the high life. Another sign of ethical decline is "insider trading" of stock by members of Congress (or their families and friends) using nonpublic information about pending corporate developments which guaranteed a rise in the prices of such stock, made known to them by corporate managers seeking their influence. Similarly, members of Congress enjoy enrichments such as discounted no fee mortgage loans, high dollar speaker fees, thinly disguised travel junkets and entertainment paid for by corporations, trade associations and the like. They use their influence to get jobs and business contracts for their friends and family members. Recent years have yielded so many corrupt schemes and activities by influence peddlers, lobbyists, corporate officers and Congressmen that most people cannot keep track of them all.

The decline in ethics among leaders has a trickle down effect as well. To quote an old proverb, the fish stinks from the head. The body politic in America today is in danger of moral and ethical rot as people in privileged positions up and down the line grab the chance to get their own "piece of the pie." Ethics in government and business is reaching an all time low. The source of the problem is the same: concentration of power in the hands of the few. Even on the local level, it is becoming more common for those who are given a little authority to imitate the big shots and "lord it" over others, forgetting the principles of ethical conduct on which this nation was founded.

❖ *Privilege vs. Equality*

The principles underlying American ethics and civility are rooted in a deeply held belief in equality. Our country has struggled over equality before. It could be said that all our great struggles, from Abolition and the Civil War to the Women's Suffrage Movement to the Civil Rights Movement, have centered on the conflict between privilege and equality. This is no less true today than when Americans fought to overthrow arrogant British colonialism, to abolish slavery, to extend the right to vote to women, or to end racial segregation.

The only difference today is that the struggle now is to break the grip of the privileged few on the power which denies equality to, and rightfully belongs to, the many. The struggle today is between plutocracy and democracy. In other societies and other times in history, struggles between the "haves" and "have nots" typically have degenerated into class warfare. Americans should not assume that "it can't happen here." If the present trends toward division persist, this great country will face grave danger.[4]

---

[4] Just as the British in America believed they had a divine right to rule the colonies, some people today believe that they are ordained to exercise power over others. The belief that power by right comes from above was overturned in the American Revolution by the idea, stated in the Declaration of Independence, that power rises from the people.

Fortunately, we have an alternative. The danger was anticipated in 1789. In that year, the revolutionaries who gave us the Declaration of Independence and the victory over the British at Yorktown also gave us the solution to our present dilemma.

The Original Bill of Rights
(National Archives)

CHAPTER THREE

THE SOLUTION

If the problem is concentration of power in the hands of the few, then the solution is to dilute the power. The way to bring Congress back down to earth is to break the lock which holds at 435 the number of Representatives in the House of Representatives. The problem we face was anticipated by the Founders in 1789. In that year, twelve proposed amendments to the brand new United States Constitution were passed by the first Congress of the United States. As required by the Constitution, these were submitted for ratification by three-fourths of the various States. Ten of the amendments were ratified in 1791. These became known as the Bill of Rights and are a sacred part of our legal system today, guaranteeing to Americans the personal freedoms from government interference for which the Founders had fought in the American Revolution.

Two of the proposed twelve amendments in the original Bill of Rights remained unratified in 1791, the first and second of them. Ratification requires adoption by a majority vote of members of the legislatures of three-fourths of the States. Of these two, the second was ratified in 1992 as the Twenty-seventh Amendment to the Constitution, 203 years after it was submitted by Congress for ratification by the States. It provides that any pay raise for members of Congress shall not take effect until election of the next succeeding Congress. This Amendment reflects the concern of the Founders that Representatives might abuse the power of their office by giving themselves extravagant pay raises. The amendment protects against such potential for abuse of power by assuring that no such pay raise can take effect until citizens have an opportunity to vote out of office the Representatives who passed it.

This leaves unratified only one more of the first twelve proposed amendments to the Constitution. It became known as Article the First because it was the first of the twelve proposed amendments submitted by Congress in the original Bill of Rights. Because it was passed by Congress with no time limit for ratification it is today, just as the Twenty-seventh Amendment was for the 203 years prior to 1992, still pending for ratification by three-fourths of the States. It reads as follows:

> Article the first… After the first enumeration required by the first article of the Constitution, there shall be one Representative for every thirty thousand, until the number shall amount to one hundred, after which the proportion shall be so regulated by Congress, that there shall be not less than one hundred Representatives, nor less than one Representative for every forty thousand persons, until the

> number of Representatives shall
> amount to two hundred; after which
> the proportion shall be so regulated by
> Congress, that there shall not be less
> than two hundred Representatives, nor
> more than one Representative for every
> fifty thousand persons.

To date, eleven States have ratified this proposed amendment: New Jersey (1789), Maryland (1789), North Carolina (1789), South Carolina (1790), New Hampshire (1790), New York (1790), Rhode Island (1790), Pennsylvania (1791), Virginia (1791), Vermont (1791), and Kentucky (1791). Since three-fourths of today's fifty States total thirty-eight, it will take ratification action by the legislatures of twenty-seven more States to adopt this proposed amendment. It is this amendment that offers the key to breaking the lock holding at 435 the number of members in the House of Representatives.

The careful reader will note that the amendment as presented for ratification contains a flaw. The ninth word from the end should have read "less" instead of "more," making the language parallel with that in the previous phrase which reads ". . . nor less than one representative for every forty thousand persons." The written historical record of the amendment's passage reflects that this mistake was the result of confusion following a conference committee meeting to reconcile the different versions of the amendment adopted by each chamber of the Congress.

This is the text of Article the First as adopted by the House of Representatives and recorded in the House Journal of its proceedings on Friday, August 21, 1789:

The House proceeded to consider the original report of the committee of eleven, consisting of seventeen articles, as now amended; whereupon the first, second, third, fourth, fifth, sixth, seventh, eighth, ninth, tenth, eleventh, twelfth, thirteenth, fourteenth, fifteenth, and sixteenth articles being again read and debated, were, upon the question severally put thereupon, agreed to by the House, as follows, two-thirds of the members present concurring, to wit:

1. After the first enumeration, there shall be one Representative for every thirty thousand, until the number shall amount to one hundred; after which, the proportion shall be so regulated by Congress, that there shall be not less than one hundred Representatives, nor less than one Representative for every forty thousand persons, until the number of Representatives shall amount to two hundred; after which, the proportion shall be so regulated, that there shall not be less than two hundred Representatives, nor less than one Representative for every fifty thousand persons.

The Journal of the Senate's proceedings, for August 25, 1789, recites the language of Article the First as quoted above and states that the proposed amendments would be taken under consideration the following Monday. The matter came up for consideration Wednesday instead, and the Senate proposed alternate language for Article the First. The matter was assigned to a committee to resolve the differences. According to the official record:

> The Committee were also of opinion it would be proper for both Houses to agree to amend the first Article, by striking out the word "less" in the last line but one, and inserting in its place the word "more", and accordingly recommend that the said Article be reconsidered for that purpose.

Journal of the Senate of the United States, Vol. 1, Page 86 (Library of Congress). The House of Representatives acceded to this change on September 24, 1789, according to the Journal of its proceedings for that day.

The Senate record for September 25, 1789, reflects the following:

> The Senate proceeded to consider the message from the House of Representatives of the 24th, with amendments to the amendments of the Senate to "Articles to be proposed to the legislatures of the several states, as amendments to the constitution of the United States;" and,

Resolved, That the Senate do concur in the amendments proposed by the House of Representatives to the amendments of the Senate.

Ordered, That the Secretary do carry a message to the House of Representatives accordingly.

Journal of the Senate of the United States, Vol. 1, Page 88 (Library of Congress). The articles of amendment were passed.

As written, the language of the proposed amendment as sent to the States for ratification contradicts its intent as passed by the House and considered by the Senate. It actually makes no sense and defeats the purpose of providing for Congress to increase the number of its members as the population of the country grew. Adopting such a change to the Constitution *as intended* by the House of Representatives, however, would have the effect of preventing the capping of the House membership at 435 members which occurred in 1929.

Even though flawed, Article the First *as intended* provides the American people today with the solution envisioned by the Founders to the dilemma facing the nation today. What will happen if we complete this piece of unfinished business of the American Revolution? Ratification of a corrected version of this first proposed amendment to the Constitution will bring about a true revolution in the government of the United States. It will restore power to the people. It will shut down the money game in Washington. It will bring an end to Pie Party politics. Upon its ratification, members of the House of Representatives will answer to the people who elected them instead of the special interests who now perpetuate their incumbency.

How will this happen? Consider these consequences of ratification. The population of the United States as of the 2010 Census was 308,745,538. If each member of the House of Representatives were elected from a congressional district numbering 50,000 people as intended by the amendment, the total membership of the House today would consist of 6,174 members. The immediate effect of such a change is a tremendous dilution of the power of each Representative. Special interest politics and lobbying to so large and diverse a body will be difficult or impossible. On the other hand, citizens of each district will be able to know personally their Representatives. People will be more involved in the process and feel that their votes count. Far away political operators and money people in Washington and New York will no longer be in control.

Fifty thousand people is the population of a small town. Suddenly politics on the federal level will become truly local. Reaching voters will no longer require Representatives to raise millions of dollars for election campaigns every two years. The problem of campaign financing goes away. Election to the House of Representatives will no longer depend on lining up contributions from special interests and wealthy donors, as it does now. It will depend instead upon developing and maintaining personal one-to-one relationships with citizen voters in the district.

The House of Representatives will be more diverse. Because each member comes from a smaller district, the whole body will reflect the diversity of races, ethnic groups, classes, interests, and opinions found in the general population. The political manipulation of Congressional redistricting which now goes on every ten years after the Census will become pointless. Most important, ordinary people will feel they have a voice and that their point of view matters.

With smaller districts comes greater personal accountability on the part of Representatives. Each Representative will therefore have a greater sense of responsibility to the people in deciding how to vote on bills allocating financial resources and regulating economic activity. Representatives will be less likely to vote for measures that cannot be funded without incurring debt. Like every other aspect of government, taxation or the decision to commit funds to war making will depend more upon the will of the people than upon Washington policy makers. Irresponsible spending will become a thing of the past in a system which fosters direct personal accountability.

The tone of political discourse will change. The intense "red state - blue state" partisanship which prevails today will be replaced by a wider variety of voices, ideas, and opinions. This is because Representatives will owe greater allegiance to the people who elected them than to party. Political discussion will no longer be characterized by the partisan bickering that prevails today. Representatives whose greater loyalty is to the people than to party will seek common ground for the common good. Political campaigns will not be driven by the "attack ads" against opponents which are today routinely paid for by shadowy political action committees ("PAC's") funded by rich contributors and special interests.

Campaigns for the United States House of Representatives will not depend upon the constant pursuit of money for reelection in which members of Congress must participate today. Campaigns for Congress will, instead, become personal and will consist of a real dialogue with voters and opponents instead of sound bites and media events. Running for the office of Representative will not depend on political or family connections and access to money. Campaigns will be more open to citizens who are willing to serve, since practically anyone will be able to go out and personally meet the voters in a district of 50,000 people.

Some may object that a House of Representatives of 6,174 members will be too large to function. Yet conventions having this many members and more commonly conduct business without difficulty. What is more, in the information age it is possible to conduct business from virtually any location. The Internet, digital telecommunications, and jet travel overcome the limitations of time and space. The House of Representatives can conduct its business in locations other than Capitol Hill. Decentralizing the House by holding hearings and deliberations elsewhere or by electronic means will go a long way toward reducing the influence and interference of special interests in the legislative process.

Nowadays people forget that the Founders who drafted the Constitution provided for a Congress which would function basically as a convention, not as a self-perpetuating institution where members would serve for decades, making careers of the office of Representative. The changes which will come about from ratification of the *intended* Article the First will restore this functional character of the House. The bottom line is that the House of Representatives will represent the people, as the Founders intended it to do. Ratification of an amendment providing for such dilution of power will, in a single stroke, make our national government truly democratic.

The first ten amendments to the Constitution, known as the Bill of Rights, were ratified to secure the fundamental freedom from tyranny for which the American Revolution was fought. The Founders knew first hand the dangers of governmental power unrestrained by written protections of the personal liberty of citizens. The also knew and experienced the dangers posed by a distant and unrepresentative legislature. The House of Commons in London passed the Stamp Act and other legislative measures which imposed burdens upon citizens of the colonies without considering their will. "No taxation without representation!" became a rallying cry of the Revolution. It could be the rallying cry of Americans today.

The taxing authority of our government was vested by the Constitution in the House of Representatives, because the Founders intended it to be the body most representative of the people among the three branches of government, but the House is no longer responsive to the will of the people. It responds to the priorities of Wall Street, the banking and finance industry, the military-industrial complex, and thousands of other special interests, and saddles citizens with unfair economic burdens. The Founders proposed the first amendment to the Constitution to address this very problem. It is no accident that they listed this proposed amendment first. Everything else in the American system depends upon preservation and maintenance of our American democracy.

The first article of amendment to the Constitution proposed by the first Congress of the United States, *as intended*, waits to solve our current crisis. Congress is hopelessly grid locked. The forces which drive the politics of money are out of control. Laws attempting to reform campaign financing or regulate lobbying amount to nothing more than band-aids. Proposals to reform the tax code are band-aids. They fail in the face of special interest politics. Attempts to jump start job creation through legislation are band-aids. The problem is systemic. It cannot be cured with band-aids. What is more, those who know fundamental change is necessary lack a clear way forward.

In recent times movements have been springing up around the *need* for real, fundamental change, but none is focused on a clear *goal*. Ratification of Article the First, *as intended*, is a clear, achievable goal. Those who participated in the framing of our system of government left us a legacy, a gift with which to address the present crisis. The time has come to ratify and adopt the Twenty-eighth Amendment to the United States Constitution based upon a corrected Article the First.

CHAPTER FOUR

THE HISTORICAL BACKGROUND

Adopting such a Twenty-eighth Amendment brings the American Revolution right down to our time. By taking a stand we become part of events which began at the birth of our country. In 1776, colonial leaders including Thomas Jefferson and John Adams gathered to draft and issue the Declaration of Independence. A shooting war broke out between the British government and the American colonists over the revolutionary ideas set forth in that document. At great personal danger and sacrifice, with death sentences looming if they failed, the leaders of the Revolution pressed on for six long years until the British were decisively defeated in 1781 at the Battle of Yorktown. It took another year for them to withdraw from garrisons in the major ports. The peace treaty came in 1783.

Already in 1781 the thirteen colonial States adopted Articles of Confederation in a first attempt to forge a national government. Lacking an executive and with no court system, the Confederation consisted mainly of a Continental Congress, composed of one house in which each State had one vote. Without the power to levy taxes or enforce its laws, the Confederation was weak. The Confederation government could not pay its bills, and in 1786 the new country was plunged into an economic depression. The States bickered with one another as currencies declined in value and people suffered.

Out of this bleak beginning emerged the call for a Constitutional Convention. The delegates sent by each State to the Convention began work on the second Monday in May, 1787, in Philadelphia. Meeting in secret throughout that hot summer, they drafted the most ingenious document of government the world has ever seen. Their final meeting took place on Monday, September 17, 1787. The members of the Convention agreed that the new Constitution would take effect when it was adopted by the legislatures of at least nine of the thirteen States. This was accomplished within the year that followed, and on April 30, 1789, George Washington became the first President under the new Constitution.

Throughout the ratification period, however, strong objections to the new Constitution were raised. These centered on the fear that the new, strong central government could abuse its power. Many expressed a concern that it could become a vehicle for establishing a nobility and monarchy. Even in the course of the Constitutional Convention, a split arose between "radicals" and "conservatives."[5] The radicals sought to plant the

---

[5] Conservatives outnumbered radicals in the Convention. Some old revolutionaries who would have joined with the radicals, notably Thomas Jefferson (who was serving as American ambassador to France) and Patrick Henry, were

revolutionary ideals of liberty and democracy in the new document. The conservatives stressed the need for stability and centralized authority. This debate continued during the ratification period after the Convention ended.

The ratification period was a time requiring much persuasion to overcome objections to the new Constitution. A series of eighty-five essays known as the "Federalist Papers" were written by Alexander Hamilton, James Madison, and John Jay in support of ratification. Published anonymously in various newspapers and journals under the name "Publius" (meaning "Citizen"), these essays shed light on the secret debates and reasoning behind the provisions in the proposed Constitution and the decisions taken on various issues at the Constitutional Convention.

Of interest here is the discussion in the Federalist Papers concerning the number of representatives to be elected to the House of Representatives. The Federalist No. 55 was authored by Alexander Hamilton or James Madison (both of whom sided with the conservatives at the Convention). At the outset, this essay recognizes the supreme importance of this hotly debated issue:

> Scarce any article, indeed, in the whole Constitution seems to be rendered more worthy of attention by the weight of character and the apparent force of

absent from the Convention. Conservatives like Alexander Hamilton and James Madison generally prevailed.

argument with which it has been assailed.

It would be a mistake to underestimate the importance of this issue, both then and now.

The essay summarizes the points raised by critics in opposition to the way this issue was resolved in the proposed Constitution. Such opponents were concerned:

> (a.) that so small a number of representatives will be an unsafe depository of the public interest;

> (b.) that the Representatives will not possess a proper knowledge of the local circumstances of their numerous constituents;

> (c.) that the Representatives will be taken from that class of citizens which will sympathize least with the feelings of the mass of the people and be most likely to aim at a permanent elevation of the few on the depression of the many; and

> (d.) that the number of Representatives will be more and more disproportionate by the increase of the people, and the obstacles which will prevent a correspondent increase in the number of Representatives.

Looking back, it seems as if those opposed to the Constitution's formulation of the number of Representatives had an uncanny ability to see the future course of events. Each of these dangers has been realized in our time.

The essay notes that, "In general it may be remarked on this subject, that no political problem is less susceptible of a precise solution than that which relates to the number most convenient for a representative legislature . . .." The author expresses a belief that:

> Nothing can be more fallacious than to found our political calculations on arithmetical principles. Sixty or seventy men may be more properly trusted with a given degree of power than six or seven. But it does not follow that six or seven hundred would be proportionably a better depository. And if we carry on the supposition to six or seven thousand, the whole reasoning ought to be reversed. The truth is, that in all cases a certain number at least seems to be necessary to secure the benefits of free consultation and discussion, and to guard against too easy a combination for improper purposes; as, on the other hand, the number ought at most to be kept within a certain limit, in order to

avoid the confusion and intemperance
of a multitude.

Obviously this conservative fear of the multitude and
avoidance of mathematical formulation was not
shared by all the Founders. The first of the proposed
amendments to the Constitution focused on this
very point.

The essayist then addresses the fourth of the
objections listed above, namely the disproportion of
population to the number of Representatives. He
projects into the future the expected increase in
number of Representatives based on population
growth, anticipating that there would be four
hundred Representatives at the expiration of fifty
years. He says:

> I take for granted here what I shall, in
> answering the fourth objection,
> hereafter show, that the number of
> representatives will be augmented from
> time to time in the manner provided by
> the Constitution. On a contrary
> supposition, I should admit the
> objection to have very great weight
> indeed.

Even applying the conservative principles expressed
in the essay, it is clear that an arbitrary cap on the
number of Representatives was not envisioned by
the Founders. The fact is that, contrary to the
expectation of the essayist, the number of
Representatives has not been augmented since 1929,

despite the fact that the population of the United States has more than doubled since then. In view of this fact, the "contrary supposition" referred to above has occurred, and the objection has been realized in our time that the House of Representatives would cease to express the will of the people because of the disproportion of Representatives to the population.

The essayist could hardly have imagined that the House of Representatives might become so corrupted by money as it is today. To him it was impossible to conceive of ". . . any sixty-five or a hundred men capable of recommending themselves to the choice of the people at large, who either desire or dare, within the short space of two years, to betray the solemn trust committed to them." He could hardly imagine Representatives serving for decades and working hand-in-glove with special interests to perpetuate their tenure in office, as happens today. Questioning from what source members of the House of Representatives might be subject to corruption, he asks:

> From what quarter can the danger proceed? Are we afraid of foreign gold? If foreign gold could so easily corrupt our federal rulers and enable them to ensnare and betray their constituents, how has it happened that we are at this time a free and independent nation?

Writing at that time, he could not have imagined the corrupting effect on government which would arise a century later from the enormous wealth of large corporations. It is this gold, not "foreign gold," that poses the danger to our system of government today. This is a danger deriving from the concentration of power in the House of Representatives that the checks and balances built into the Constitution do not address.

Other public voices at the time the Constitution was submitted for ratification clearly recognized its defects and the dangers of abuse of power. Recognizing the need for an effective central government, they did not oppose ratification. They gave the new Constitution their assent with reservations. Notable among these was Patrick Henry, famous then as he is now for his declaration at the moment of revolutionary truth in 1775, "I know not what course others may take, but as for me, give me liberty, or give me death!"

Patrick Henry was a leader in the fight to amend the new Constitution. With true revolutionary fervor, he did not assume that those who went into government would be good and high minded. In the debates over ratification of the Constitution in the Virginia convention, he stated:

> The Constitution is said to have beautiful features; but when I come to examine these features, sir, they appear to me to be horribly frightful. Among other deformities, it has an awful squinting; it squints toward monarchy. And does this not raise indignation in

the breast of every true American?
Your president may easily become king.
. . . Where are your checks in this
government? Your strongholds will be
in the hands of your enemies. It is on a
supposition that your American
governors shall be honest, that all the
good qualities of this government are
founded; but its defective and
imperfect construction puts it in their
power to perpetuate the worst of
mischiefs, should they be bad men.
And, sir, would not all the world, from
the eastern to the western hemispheres,
blame our distracted folly in resting our
rights upon the contingency of our
rulers being good or bad?[6]

In stark contrast to the sentiment expressed in the
Federalist No. 55, Patrick Henry clearly foresaw the
danger which we face today.

The absence in the proposed Constitution of
written guarantees of personal rights and freedoms
was considered by advocates of amending the
Constitution to be an abandonment of the ideals of
the Revolution. Similarly, they decried the lack of
guarantees against a self-perpetuating monarchy or
tyranny in the office of the President (what we today

---

[6] Elliot, Jonathan, *The Debates in the Several State Conventions on
the Adoption of the Federal Constitution,* Philadelphia, 1876,
quoted in Tyler, Moses Coit, *Patrick Henry,* Houghton, Mifflin
& Co., New York, 1898, p. 327.

might call the "imperial presidency"), as well as concentration of power in the House of Representatives with no provision to assure that it would remain subject to the will of the people.

These were ideals for which men and women had fought and died in the Revolution. They were not taken lightly. The old revolutionaries, believing these ideals were being compromised or forgotten in the push for ratification of the Constitution, took a stand for amendment of the document in order to secure these ideals. Thomas Jefferson, writing from Paris to a friend on February 2, 1788, said:

> I own it astonishes me to find such a change wrought in the opinions of our countrymen since I left them, as that three fourths of them should be contented to live under a system which leaves to their governors the power of taking from them the trial by jury in civil cases, freedom of religion, freedom of the press, freedom of commerce, the habeas corpus laws, and of yoking them with a standing army. That is a degeneracy in the principles of liberty to which I had given four centuries, instead of four years.[7]

---

[7] Bancoft, George, *History of the Formation of the Constitution of the United States of America,* New York, 1882, quoted in Tyler, Moses Coit, *Patrick Henry,* Houghton, Mifflin & Co., New York, 1898, p. 330.

Those who had such reservations also recognized the need to establish a new national government, so they chose to support ratification of the Constitution with a clear intention to use the mechanism for amendment provided in the Constitution to correct its deficiencies. Patrick Henry, speaking before the ratification convention in Virginia, said:

> My head, my hand, and my heart shall be at liberty to retrieve the loss of liberty and remove the defects of that system in a constitutional way. I wish not to go to violence, but will wait, with hopes that the spirit which predominated in the Revolution is not yet gone, nor the cause of those who are attached to the Revolution yet lost. I shall therefore patiently wait in expectation of seeing that government changed, so as to be compatible with the safety, liberty, and happiness of the people.[8]

After the Virginia ratification convention adjourned, James Madison wrote to George Washington as follows:

> Mr. H---y declared, previous to the final question, that although he should submit as a quiet citizen, he should

---

[8] Elliot, Jonathan, *The Debates in the Several State Conventions on the Adoption of the Federal Constitution,* Philadelphia, 1876, quoted in Tyler, Moses Coit, *Patrick Henry,* Houghton, Mifflin & Co., New York, 1898, p. 332.

seize the first moment that offered for shaking off the yoke in a constitutional way. I suspect the plan will be to encourage two thirds of the legislatures in the task of undoing the work; or to get a Congress appointed in the first instance that will commit suicide on their own authority.[9]

Patrick Henry
(Library of Congress Collection)

[9] Madison, James, *Letters and Other Writings*, Philadelphia, 1867, quoted in Tyler, Moses Coit, *Patrick Henry*, Houghton, Mifflin & Co., New York, 1898, p. 343-4.

Madison, ironically, would himself play a key role in the events which led to adoption of the first ten amendments to the Constitution which came to be known as the Bill of Rights.

Patrick Henry did not wait long to make good on his declared intention to correct the deficiencies of the Constitution. When the Virginia Assembly convened in 1788, he was present as an elected delegate. Unlike the convention to ratify the Constitution, in the Virginia Assembly Patrick Henry held sway. His first and only order of business was passage of a resolution for submission to the first federal Congress calling for a new constitutional convention among the States. By that time, his views on the deficiencies of the new Constitution were well known and were widely shared by many old revolutionaries in other States.

The Virginia resolution calling for a new constitutional convention posed a problem for the first Congress of the United States. Borrowing Madison's words, voting for a new constitutional convention could be seen as institutional suicide for the first Congress convened under the new Constitution. Yet Congress could not ignore the resolution from Virginia and the strong sentiment for amendment of the Constitution which lay behind it in Virginia and other States. A real possibility existed that two-thirds of the thirteen legislatures might be marshaled to convene such a new constitutional convention if Congress itself did not

James Madison
(Library of Congress Collection)

act. Several months into the legislative term, as these sentiments percolated in the new republic, the first House of Representatives found a way around the problem.

Under the guidance of Madison (who by this time had gained appointment to the first Congress as a Representative from Virginia), the House adopted seventeen proposed amendments to the new Constitution and sent them to the Senate for approval. The Senate adopted twelve of them; these became the original Bill of Rights. By 1791, ten of these amendments had been ratified by three-fourths of the States. In 1992, the eleventh was ratified by three-fourths of the States.

The last remaining amendment sent to the States for approval in the original Bill of Rights was the one at the top of the list in 1789: Article the First, the amendment to apportion the number of Representatives according to the population determined by the Census. The clear intention was to make the House of Representatives the most democratic institution in the federal government. By diluting the power granted to it among a large number of Representatives and providing for two year terms of service, the House was conceived as the body most responsive to the will of the people. It was because the Founders saw it as having this guarantee that they invested it with such enormous powers.

As we have seen, this intention has been foiled by the Apportionment Act of 1929, fixing the number of Representatives at 435, and by the other historical forces which have served to render the House unresponsive, rather than responsive, to the will of the people. In our time we are witnessing the dangerous forces of privilege, corruption, and abuse of power of which the old revolutionaries warned at the birth of the new nation.

The time has now come to complete the work of the Revolution by forging a movement to ratify a corrected Article the First as the Twenty-eighth Amendment to the United States Constitution.

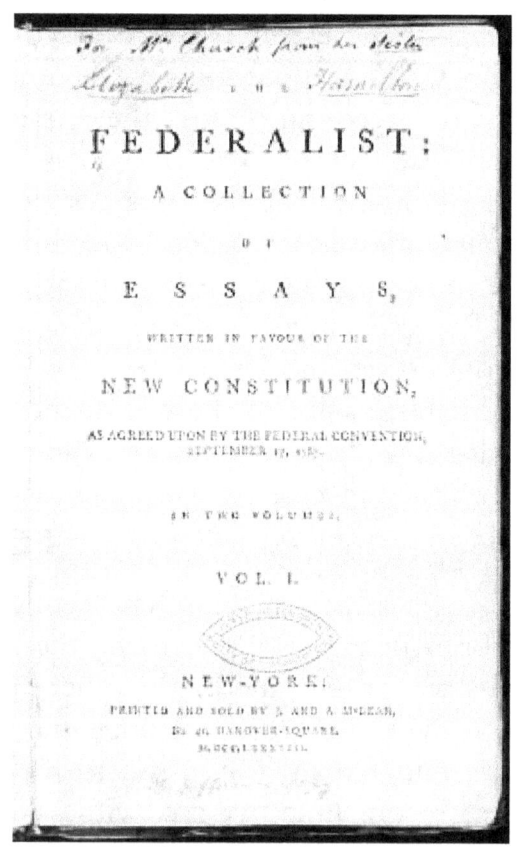

Thomas Jefferson's Copy of *The Federalist*
(Library of Congress Collection)

CHAPTER FIVE

WHAT TO DO

Americans who want to take back their government have a way forward. The template for ratifying the Twenty-eighth Amendment can be found in the steps taken to ratify the Twenty-seventh Amendment. What is called for is a citizen movement aimed at Congress and the legislatures of the several States. This is how the process works.

If the error in the proposed Amendment can be corrected, by court action or by the current chief clerk of the House, the great advantage for ordinary citizens is this: it will not be necessary in this case to clear the first and greatest hurdle for amendment of the Constitution. In that case, there would be no requirement to propose the amendment and seek approval by Congress of its submission to the States or to petition the States to call for a constitutional convention. That step has already been taken by our forefathers. We need only to get the legislatures of twenty-seven more States to ratify the corrected amendment. In the case of such a correction, the Twenty-eighth Amendment will be a gift handed down to us from the first American Revolution. When it is ratified, we will witness a revolution in our time; we will see the American Revolution through to completion.

The Twenty-seventh Amendment was ratified in 1992 as the result of just such a citizen movement as is called for in this instance. Submitted to the States for ratification in 1789, along with the other eleven amendments in the Bill of Rights, it received little attention until 1982, when an undergraduate student at the University of Texas in Austin named Gregory Watson wrote a paper about it. Watson suggested that it would be a good thing to pursue ratification of the amendment, preventing members of Congress from benefiting from a pay raise on which they had themselves voted until the people had a chance to express their will in a subsequent congressional election. He sparked a campaign of letter writing to State legislatures which had not yet ratified the amendment. Ten years later, the Twenty-seventh Amendment was ratified.

Clearing the way for such a movement was the decision of the Supreme Court of the United States in the historic case of *Coleman v. Miller*, 307 U.S. 433 (1939), holding that the requirements for ratifying a constitutional amendment are political in nature and, therefore, are outside the scope of its jurisdiction. Under that case, any amendment which has been submitted to the States without a specified deadline for ratification can be ratified by a three-fourths majority of the States at any time. The proposed Twenty-eighth Amendment to the Constitution was submitted by the first Congress to the States without any deadline or time limit for ratification. It is, therefore, still pending and may be adopted any time twenty-seven more State legislatures act to ratify it.

If the one word error in the pending amendment cannot be corrected, the process of passing the amendment through Congress and submitting it for passage by three-fourths of the State legislatures will have to be done again. This would require persuading two-thirds of the members of Congress to adopt it or a call by two-thirds of the State legislatures to convene a Constitutional Convention.

Powerful voices will be raised against a movement to ratify the proposed Twenty-eighth Amendment. Large financial interests will be threatened. The fundamentals of the Washington power game will be changed. The power and privilege of the few will be in jeopardy. A well financed media campaign will be mounted against this idea. Powerful leaders in government and business will caution us against the dangers of so radical a change. Some political commentators will ridicule it as naive or unworkable.

The greater the outcry against it from those who are entrenched in the present system, the more we can be sure it is democratic and revolutionary. Know this: the most powerful forces in America cannot resist the will of the people. A well organized grassroots campaign in each State will lead inevitably to its ratification. This is how politics in America ultimately gets done. If members of Congress or State legislators do not see the importance of this change, they can be voted out of office and replaced by legislators who will. People who care about this great nation will rally around this cause. You can organize in your own State and join hands with like minded people in other States to bring about this change in our system of government. What to do is this: organize.

Such great work has been accomplished before many times in the American experience. America has a great tradition of grassroots activism. No one need tell Americans how to organize. You will be participating in a process of change and renewal that began in the American Revolution. Citizens today follow in illustrious footsteps in joining the campaign to make this happen.

In colonial times, the original revolutionaries advocated for democracy. They held the will of the people to be sacred against opponents who feared "the mob." This same fear of the mob, the fear that the system will be out of control, undoubtedly will be raised against this movement. To borrow the famous words of Franklin D. Roosevelt, however, we really have nothing to fear in this instance but fear itself.

The Founders were wise in the ways of government and human nature. We can put faith in their understanding of the dangers posed by concentration of power in the hands of the few. Beyond this, we need not act on faith alone, because we have seen first hand just what happens when the few are permitted to hold sway over the many. Consider this: the alternative to changing the system is continuation of the present system until our nation is bankrupt and truly out of control. At that point, violence will prevent orderly change, and this great chance to restore democracy to our system of government will have been lost.

After ratification of the Twenty-eighth Amendment, the self-organizing principles at work in a free and democratic nation will assure that the work of Congress gets done. Representatives in so large a body will form coalitions around the various issues presented to it for consideration. Debate and dialogue will be aided by advantages of technology not dreamed of in years past. The House of Representatives will be decentralized. Its focus will be directed at the will of the people. The Pie Party will be over.

On the occasions when it needs to convene as a body, the House of Representatives will need a new and larger chamber. This is nothing new. In the earliest days of the republic, the House met in a small chamber in the Capitol building, and the Supreme Court sat in the Capitol building as well. Today, the House and Senate are no longer confined to the Capitol building, but have off-site office buildings joined to the Capitol by a system of underground passageways and tunnels. The Supreme Court now has its own building across the street. The larger House of Representatives may well need its own hall to accommodate all its members. Such changes are easily achieved.

The first step is to form a statewide organization in each of the States to secure ratification and to organize local chapters in each community. These groups and chapters, organized simply around a name such as "The Article the First Movement," will draw support from citizens across the political spectrum. They will not serve any particular partisan cause or ideology. Their only function will be to build grassroots support for ratification and focus contact with the State legislatures where ratification is needed, or to pressure Congress to approve a corrected version of the amendment.

To those who fear a future America in which the people really do rule, let us ask this: is our present situation the better way? Is a system which, in the moment of truth, brought us to the edge of economic meltdown the better way? Is political grid lock the better way? Concentration of power in the hands of the few has brought us to the brink of disaster. The danger persists. Sincere people recognize that we cannot continue on our present course much longer.

This movement needs to be moderate and law-abiding. The change to be wrought will be revolutionary and far reaching in its effect. Yet the methods to be used are peaceful and are sanctioned by the Constitution itself. This must be a nonpartisan movement, welcoming to all, promoting lawful action to give a greater voice to each American regardless of his or her political ideology or persuasion.

Make no mistake: the movement to ratify the Twenty-eighth Amendment will bring on a fight.

Those who will oppose it are well heeled and well connected. With determination, however, the American people will prevail.

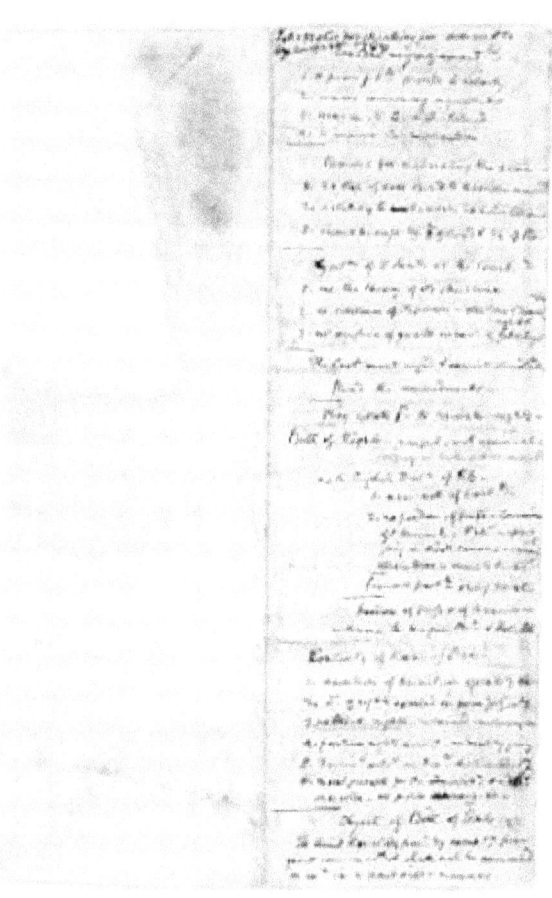

Madison's Notes for Speech to Congress
Introducing the Bill of Rights, 1789
(Library of Congress Collection)

EPILOGUE

A FINAL WORD

In 1776, at the dawn of the American Revolution, John Adams observed to his friend Richard Lee as follows:

> You and I, dear friend, have been sent into life at a time when the greatest lawgivers of antiquity would have wished to live. How few of the human race have ever enjoyed an opportunity of making an election of government . . . for themselves or for their children.

Much the same can be said about the present generation of Americans. Adams, like the other Founders of the Republic, had a strong sense of destiny in the work which was done by them.

America today stands at a crossroads. The nation faces a dangerous passage. If present tendencies continue, our country will become a plutocracy.[10]

---

[10] There are many today who believe this has already occurred. *See, e.g.,* Phillips, Kevin, *Wealth and Democracy: A Political History of the American Rich,* Broadway Books (2002), Introduction at xv (". . . the essence of plutocracy, fulfilled by 2000, has been the determination and ability of wealth to reach beyond its own realm of money and control politics and government as well."). An October 2005 Citigroup

Plutocracy is defined by Webster's as government by the wealthy, or a controlling class of the wealthy. Every American should ask: is this to be the end of the Great Experiment which began in 1776 with the American Revolution? The answer must be a resounding "No!"

The colonists in the Revolution rallied around the slogan, "No taxation without representation!" They rose up against the offense of being taxed by Parliament in London, a remote, out of touch legislature which they had no power to vote in or out of office. It was this offense which led to acts of resistance like the Boston Tea Party.

Few Americans today feel that the House of Representatives represents them when it enacts a tax code thousands of pages long with provisions and loopholes designed to favor the wealthy minority over the majority of the people. Many American corporations and wealthy individuals pay little in taxes, or even no taxes, while the shrinking middle class carries the burden. Most Americans consider Congress to be out of touch with the plight of ordinary citizens. They feel powerless to vote incumbents out of office. Americans, in short, are once again subject to taxation without

---

memorandum which circulated widely via the Internet (until the banking giant suppressed it on grounds of copyright violation) coined the term "plutonomy" to describe the current American economic system, in which the richest one percent of households has greater financial worth than the bottom ninety-five percent of households put together.

representation. Americans must once again win the Revolution.

The stakes in this fight are high. The American system of government and the ideals enshrined in the Declaration of Independence are a beacon of hope to the whole world. Generations of Americans have fought, and many have died, for these ideals. Americans owe it not only to themselves and their children, but to the whole world and posterity to hold true to those ideals. This is a time of destiny for the American people. This is a chance to participate personally in the American Revolution. Your decision to act now will make a difference.